KETO ~~~~

COOK BOOK FOR BEGINNERS

SHAHRUKH AKHTAR

SHARK PUBLICATIONS

11. *Vanilla ice cream*

12. Keto blueberry muffins

13. Pumpkin pecan pie ice

14 Keto vanilla pound cake

15. Keto mocha ice cream

16 Keto chocolate mug

17. Butterscotch sea salt ice cream

18 No Bake Low Carb Lemon Strawberry Cheesecake

19. Chocolate Chunk Avocado Ice Cream

20. Strawberry Rhubarb Ice Cream

21. Keto oven-baked Brie cheese

22. Avocado pops

23 Pecan cheesecake

24. Lemon ice cream

25 Coconut cookies

26.Almond Roll with Pumpkin Cream Cheese Filling

27. Orange Cake Balls

28 Carrot Cake Keto Balls

29. Sugar Free "Mounds" Fudge

30. Nuts fat bombs with apples

31. Granola fat bombs

32. Macadamia Nut Fat Bomb

33. Fat bomb fudge

34. Peanut butter white chocolate cups

WHY I WROTE THIS BOOK

I wrote this book so that I can share the knowledge of Ketogenic diet with everyone who wants to lose weight and live a healthy lifestyle. This book will help you to understand what is ketogenic diet and how your body acts in keto state. There are so many myths and doubts related to Ketogenic diet, all doubts will be resolved in this book.

This book will give you complete information about the followings-

What is ketogenic diet?

Different types of ketogenic diets.

Benefits of ketogenic diet.

What to eat on ketogenic diet.

Getting started with Ketogenic diet.

How to reach Ketosis.

How to know if you have achieved ketosis.

Exercise on Ketogenic diet.

Ketogenic diet Macros.

Dangers of Ketogenic diet.

Keto Flu.

Keto Recipies.

CHAPTER 1

WHAT IS KETOGENIC DIET?

I am sure all of you have heard about Ketogenic diet. Everyone is talking about Keto diet these days.

"The life changing diet"

"Diet which gives you enormous energy"

"Diet on which you never get hungry" etc.

But is Ketogenic diet really that effective? Let's find out what Ketogenic diet really is.

Ketogenic diet is a diet in which you consume high amounts of fats, moderate amount of proteins and very low amount of carbohydrates. After eating high fats, moderate proteins and really low carbohydrates for few days, our body achieves a metabolic state known as Ketosis.

When our body is in Ketosis state, than our liver produces small fuel molecules called Ketones. Ketones are used by the body as energy source when there is low blood sugar (glucose).

Why blood sugar gets low in this diet?

Our body converts carbohydrates into glucose; Carbohydrates are broken down into blood sugar because glucose enters your bloodstream and increases your blood sugar level.

When blood sugar level increases, than insulin is produced by pancreas and this is how body stores sugar for energy. Sugar is absorbed by cells and this is how your insulin level stabilizes itself.

Your body's blood sugar is consistently high when you eat lots of carbohydrates .

Ketones

When your blood sugar levels are low than your liver produces Ketones, which are used as alternative source of energy by the body.

On Ketogenic diet, your whole body runs by Ketones. It switches its energy source entirely on fats. Your body burns fat dramatically because your insulin levels become really low. Your body's fat stores becomes easily accessible and it becomes really easy to burn them off.

The purpose of ketogenic diet is to turn your body into fat burning state, where it takes energy from fats for fuel. Ketosis is nothing but the survival mechanism of our body, it helps our body to run on fats when there is no food available.

Weight loss is not the only benefit that you will experience on this diet; there are many more benefits of this diet. To name a few, you will feel less hungry on this diet, your energy levels will become really high, it will increase your alertness and will keep you focused.

CHAPTER 2

DIFFERENT TYPES OF KETOGENIC DIETS

There are total of three types of ketogenic diet, each one is little different from another. Test all and see which suits you the best.

Standard Ketogenic diet

This is the most popular type of ketogenic diet. This diet is high in fats, moderate in proteins and very low in carbohydrates. This diet is best for those who do really low intensity activities.

In this diet you are allowed to consume really low amount of carbohydrates generally around 20-50 grams. If you go above 50 grams of carbohydrates per day, than you might get out of ketosis.

Carbohydrate limits are different for different people, but the general approach is to avoid breads, pastas, fruits (high in carbohydrates) and everything that includes high amount of carbohydrates.

You are allowed to have green vegetables, seeds, nuts which are low in carbohydrates on this diet; they will be the primary source of carbohydrates that you will take in Standard Ketogenic diet.

Targeted Ketogenic diet

In targeted ketogenic diet you consume carbohydrates around your workouts; usually 30-60 minutes before a workout, so that your workouts performance does not go down and high intensity exercises are performed effectively and efficiently. Rest of the time you follow standard ketogenic diet. This diet helps in promotion of glycogen replenishment.

This diet will be best suited for these individuals :

1. Athletes that need carbohydrates to improve their exercise performance.

2. People who are new to exercise programme.

Cyclical Ketogenic diet

Cyclical ketogenic diet combines carbohydrates loading days and standard ketogenic diet. This diet is best suited for those who perform really heavy workouts and high intensity trainings. This diet is for athletes and bodybuilders, since high intensity is required in their workouts and their performance should not suffer with ketogenic diet. They do require carbohydrates to maintain high quality workouts.

They are allowed to have carbohydrates to replenish themselves for once or twice a week, so that they get the fuel for their trainings.

Cyclical ketogenic diet is not like targeted ketogenic diet, the main goal in targeted ketogenic diet is to keep blood sugar and muscles glycogen at a moderate level. The goal of Cyclical Ketogenic diet is to completely replenish glycogen during fuel loading and to deplete glycogen and raise ketone levels between carbohydrate charges.

CHAPTER 3

BENEFITS OF KETOGENIC DIET

Ketogenic diet is more than just a diet, it is a lifestyle.

When you hear people say Ketogenic diet changed their life's forever, they are not kidding; They really mean it.

Weight loss

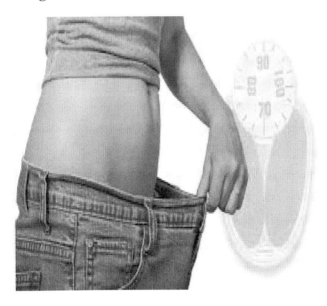

Ketogenic diet is the best diet available today in the market. With ketogenic diet your fat loss happens really quickly in a healthy manner because your body is using your fat reserves for energy even while doing your mundane tasks. You don't feel hungry on this diet. Your body turns itself into a fat burning machine.

Blood sugar level

Diabetes is caused because your body is not able to handle high insulin levels. Ketogenic diet automatically lowers your blood sugar levels because you are not taking in carbohydrates which turns into glucose and increases your blood sugar stream.

Keto diet is really very helpful and effective for those suffering from diabetes.

Ketogenic diet controls your blood sugar levels and gives you more control in life.

Mental focus

Ketogenic diet gives you a laser sharp focus; you are not distracted with your thoughts. Your mental performance increases while on ketogenic diet. Many people follow keto lifestyle just because they want to increase their mental focus and wants to achieve success; they are perfectly fit but still follow this diet.

Ketones are really great fuel source for your brain and this is the reason why your mental performance increases while being on Ketogenic diet. Increase of fatty acids really enhances your mental focus.

Increase in energy

As you already know that Keto turns fats into energy source but do you know that while being on Keto, your energy levels increases massively because when your body which was running by glucose, needed constant supply of glucose but on ketosis your body functions using ketones which are more reliable sources of energy.

Better appetite control

When your body runs on glucose, you often find yourself hungry all the time but on Ketogenic diet your appetite is much more controlled and you don't feel hungry all the time because fats are naturally more satisfying and they end up leaving our body in satiated state for much longer. Now you can say goodbye to random cravings which you used to feel all the time being on a normal diet.

Epilepsy

Since 1900, Ketogenic diet is used to cure epilepsy. Today also it is the most common way to cure children suffering from epilepsy.

Biggest benefit of ketogenic diet for those who are suffering from epilepsy is that it allows them to take few medicines.

Cholesterol and blood pressure

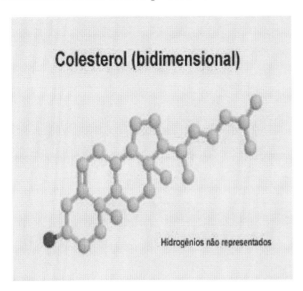

Ketogenic diet improves your triglyceride levels and cholesterol levels. The benefit of this is that there is very less toxic build up in the arteries which allows blood to flow throughout the body as it should flow.

Ketogenic diet increases your HDL (good cholesterol) and decreases LDL (bad cholesterol).

According to various researches, it has been found that low carbohydrates diet improves your blood pressure.

Excess weight gain most often leads to blood pressure issues. With ketogenic diet you lose all your unwanted fat, so it naturally improves your blood pressure.

Insulin resistance

Type II diabetes is caused due to insulin resistance. Ketogenic diet naturally lowers insulin levels of individual to healthy ranges, so that they are no longer in the group of people that are on the cusp of acquiring diabetes.

Acne

Ketogenic diet improves your skin too. A lot of people have experienced ther benefit of a clear and healthy skin.

CHAPTER 4

WHAT TO EAT ON KETOGENIC DIET

Keto diet can be tough in starting but it becomes really easy after few days, when it becomes a lifestyle. On Keto diet, you cannot eat everything you want but with time, craving for those unhealthy foods will disappear and you will not feel the urge to eat unhealthy foods again.

And even if the urge doesn't disappear, than there are many alternative to those foods in Ketogenic diet.

On Ketogenic diet, you are not allowed carbohydrates from junk foods and you are not allowed to have healthy carbohydrates also such as brown rice, brown bread, whole wheat etc.

The goal of this diet is to turn your body into fat burning machine by taking its energy from fats.

Foods to avoid on Ketogenic diet

GRAINS

Yes, all grains even the healthy ones. Grains contains lots of carbohydrates and they will stop your body to reach the state of ketosis.

GRAINS	CARBOHYDRATES	PROTEINS	FATS
WHEAT(1slice of bread)	14G	3G	1G
BARLEY	44G	4G	1G
OATS	26G	6G	3G
RICE	45G	5G	2G
RYE	15G	3G	1G
CORN	32G	4G	1G
QUINOA	39G	8G	4G
MILLET	41G	6G	2G
SORGHUM	39G	5G	1G
BULGUR	33G	5.6G	.4G
AMARANTH	46G	9G	4G
SPROUTED GRAINS	15G	4G	.5G
BUCKWHEAT	33G	6G	1G

BEANS

Beans are healthy for those on a regular diet but they are not suitable for ketogenic diet.

BEANS AND LEGUMES	CARBOHYDRATES	PROTEIN	FAT
KIDNEY BEANS	18.5G	7G	0.75G
CHICK PEAS	20G	6G	2G
BLACK BEANS	23G	7G	0.5G
LENTILS	19G	8G	0G
GREEN PEAS	14G	4G	0G
LIMA BEANS	19G	6G	0G
PINTO BEANS	20G	7G	0G
WHITE BEANS	22G	8G	0G
CHANNELLINI BEANS	18G	6G	0.5G
FAVA BEANS	17G	6G	0G
BLACK EYED PEAS	14G	2G	0G

FRUITS

Fruits are very healthy on normal diet but they are not allowed on keto diet because they contain high amounts of sugars which are considered as simple carbohydrates.

FRUITS	CARBOHYDRATES	PROTEIN	FAT
BANANA	18.5G	0.9G	0.2G
PINEAPPLE	18G	1G	0G
PAPAYA	15G	0.9G	0.2G
APPLE	22G	0G	0G
ORANGE	17G	1G	0.3G
GRAPES	27G	1G	0G
MANGOS	50G	3G	1G
TANGERINES	12G	1G	0G
ALL FRUIT JUICES	26G	2G	0G
FRUIT SMOOTHIES	VARIES	VARIES	VARIES
DRIED DATES,	57G	2G	0G
FRUIT SYRUPS	15G	0G	0G

STARCHY VEGETABLES

The simple rule is to avoid vegetables that grow beneath the ground and consume more of leafy vegetables.

STARCHY VEGETABLES	CARBOHYDRATES	PROTEIN	FAT
SWEET POTATOES	14G	1G	0G
YAMS	19G	1G	0G
POTATOES	28G	3G	0.3G
CARROTS	6G	1G	0G
PARSNIPS	15G	1G	0.3G
PEAS	14G	4G	0G
YUCCA	39G	1.5G	0G
CORN	32G	4G	1G
CHERRY TOMATOES	6G	1.3G	0.3G

SUGARS

Sugars are a complete no-no on ketogenic diet, they will get you out of ketosis really quickly.

SUGARS	CARBOHYDRATES	PROTEINS	FAT
HONEY	17G	0G	0G
AGAVE NECTAR	14G	0G	0G
MAPLE SYRUP	14G	0G	0G
RAW SUGAR	12G	0G	0G
TURBINADO SUGAR	12G	0G	0G
CORN SYRUP	14G	0G	0G
CANE SUGAR	12G	0G	0G

MILK AND LOW FAT DAIRY

Full fat dairy are ok on ketogenic diet but avoid low fat dairy products because they are high in carbohydrates.

MILK AND LOW FAT DAIRY	CARBOHYDRATES	PROTEINS	FATS
MILK	12G	8G	5G
SHREDDED CHEESE	2G	14G	18G
FAT FREE BUTTER SUBSTITUTES	0.63G	0G	0.4G
LOW FAT CREAM CHEESE	1G	2G	2.6G
EVAPORATED SKIM MILK	14G	10G	0.2G
LOW FAT WHIPPED TOPPING	3G	0G	0G
FAT FREE OR LOW FAT YOGURTS	16G	0G	0G

FACTORY FARMED ANIMAL PRODUCTS

Avoid grain fed meats and dairy because they are lower in nutrients.

Factory farmed fish is really high in mercury, that's why you should avoid it.

Packaged sausages and processed meats usually contains nitrates which are very harmful and can even cause cancer.

Unhealthy (inflammatory) oils

Unhealthy inflammatory oils should be avoided because they are not good for health. Some of them are as following –

SOYBEAN OIL	CANOLA OIL
CORN OIL	SESAME OIL
CORN OIL	SUNFLOWER OIL
GRAPESEED OIL	SAFFLOWER OIL

DRINKS TO AVOID

Drinks should be avoided in all types of diets because they all contain really high calories and you still feel hungry after drinking them. Best drink is water, drink it as much as you want. On keto diet you have to be really careful about what you are drinking.

ALCOHOL

ALCOHOL	CARBS	PROTEINS	FATS
BEER	12.7G	1.6G	0G
WINE	14G	0.2G	0G
COCKTAILS	5G	0.1G	0G
JUICES	12G	0G	0G
SYRUPS	12G	0G	0G
SODAS	12G	0G	0G
FLAVORED LIQUORS	3-6G	0G	0G

Alcohol can slow down your fat loss, that's why it is best to stay away from alcohol. Alcohol drinks do have carbohydrates.

If you really want to drink and cannot give up on alcohol than go for hard liquor, it is low in carbohydrates. Even though it is made from carbohydrates only but the sugars gets converted into ethyl alcohol during fermentation and distillation process.

SWEETENED AND SUGARY BEVERAGES

Sugary beverages should be avoided at all costs, they are full of carbohydrates and includes high calories in them.

SWEETENED BEVERAGES	CARBOHYDRATES	PROTEIN	FATS
SWEETENED SODAS	36G	0.2G	0G
ALL DIET SODAS	0G	0G	0G
FRUIT JUICES	18G	0.1G	0G
FRUIT SMOOTHIES	34G	0.8G	0.2G
COFFEE OR TEA	VARIES	VARIES	VARIES
MILK AND DAIRY	VARIES	VARIES	VARIES

PROCESSED OR PACKAGED FOODS

Not only are they unhealthy but they also contains extra sugars, carbohydrates, trans fats, preservatives and other junk. Avoid foods mentioned below.

PACKAGED FOODS	CARBOHYDRATES	PROTEINS	FATS
COOKIES	30G	2G	10G
MASRGARINES	0.63G	0G	0.4G
CANDIES	9G	0G	0G
ICECREAMS	2G	4.7G	14.2G
WHEAT GLUTEN	2G	46G	1G

And beware of foods that state themselves as low in carbohydrates, they may be low in one serving size but one serving size doesn't make you full, you still feel hungry after taking one serving size. Marketers are really very smart and they do whatever they can to sell their products, use your brain and don't fall in traps like these.

ARTIFICIAL SWEETENER

Artificial sweeteners can cause cravings in you, they can make you hungry and crave for sugars, they also affect blood sugar levels.

EQUAL	SPLENDA
ACESULFAME	SACCHARIN
ASPARTAME	SUCRALOSE

CONDIMENTS

It is best to make condiments on your own, so that you are aware of what ingredients are getting used. Some of the condiments to avoid are as follow-

MADE WITH UNHEALTHY OILS
CONTAINING ADDED SUGARS
LABELLED LOW FAT

FOODS TO EAT ON KETOGENIC DIET

FATS AND OILS

Fats will be the most important nutrient of your diet.

Saturated fats. Some examples are butter, ghee, coconut oil and lard.

Monounsaturated fats. Some examples are olive, avocado and macadamia nut oils.

Polyunsaturated fat. Realize the difference. Natural polyunsaturated fats in animal protein and oily fish are perfect for you and you should eat them. Polyunsaturated fats, which are processed in heart-healthy margarine spreads are bad for you.

Some ketogenic diet foods that are ideal for fats and oils (organic and grass-fed sources are preferred):

Fatty Fish
Animal Fat (non-hydrogenated)
Lard
Tallow
Avocados
Egg Yolks
Macadamia/Brazil Nuts
Butter/Ghee
Mayonnaise
Coconut Butter
Cocoa Butter
Olive Oil
Coconut Oil
Avocado Oil
Macadamia Oil

Beef.

Minced meat, steak, roast and meat stew. Stay with larger cuts if possible

Fish.

Preferably, you can eat all types of fish, such as catfish, cod, plaice, halibut, mackerel, mahi-mahi, salmon, snapper, trout and tuna.

Seafood,

Mussels, oysters, lobsters, crabs, scallops, clams and cuttlefish.

Whole eggs.

Try to get them from the local market as much as possible. You can prepare them in different ways, such as fries, stuffed, cooked, poached and scrambled eggs.

Pork meat.

Minced meat, pork loin, pork chops, filet, mignon and ham. Watch for added sugar and try to stay with larger cuts.

Poultry.

Chicken, duck, quail, pheasant etc.

Offal's / organ.

Heart, liver, kidney and tongue. Offal is one of the best sources of vitamins / nutrients.

Hazelnut butter.

Opt for unsweetened natural nuts and try to stick with fatter versions like almond butter and macadamia butter. Legumes (peanuts) are rich in omega-6, so watch out for overconsumption.

Other meats.

Calf, goat, lamb, turkey and other game. Stay with larger cuts if possible.

Bacon and Sausage.

Check the labels for something that has sugars or if it contains additional fillers. Do not worry about nitrates.

PROTEIN SOURCE	CARBOHYDRATES	PROTEINS	FATS
BEEF (4 OZ)	0G	21G	24G
Rib eye steak (4 oz.)	0G	28G	26G
Bacon (4 oz.)	0G	14G	50G
Pork chop (4 oz.)	0G	31G	20G
Chicken thigh (4 oz.)	0G	19G	22G
Chicken breast (4 oz.)	0G	25G	2G
Salmon (4 oz.)	0G	24G	16G
Ground lamb (4 oz.)	0G	20G	28G
Liver (4 oz.)	0G	20G	6G
EGG	0G	7G	6G
Almond butter (2 tbsp.)	5G	7G	17G

VEGETABLES AND FRUITS

Vegetables are important part of ketogenic diet but some vegetables are high in sugars and we should avoid such vegetables.

Best vegetables for ketogenic are low in carbohydrates and high in nutrition.

Majority of fruits are high in sugars but there are few which are perfect for ketogenic diet.

Below is the list of vegetables and fruits that you can eat in ketogenic diet.

KETGENIC VEGETABLES AND FRUITS (6OZ)	CARBOHYDRATES	PROTEINS	FATS
Cabbage	5G	3G	0G
Cauliflower	5G	4G	0G
Broccoli	6G	4G	0G
Spinach	1G	5G	0G
Romaine Lettuce	1G	3G	0G
Green Bell Pepper	4G	2G	0G
Baby Bella Mushrooms	5G	7G	0G
Green Beans	5G	3G	0G
Yellow Onion	11G	1G	0G
Blackberries	7G	1G	0G
Raspberries	7G	1G	0G

DAIRY PRODUCTS

Not all dairy products are Keto friendly but those high in fats and low in carbohydrates are perfect for Ketogenic diet. Below is the list of dairy foods you can consume on ketogenic diet.

Keto Dairy Source (1oz)	Carbohydrates	Proteins	Fats
Heavy cream	0G	0G	13G
Greek yogurt	2G	4G	2G
Mayonnaise	1G	1G	21G
Half n' half	2G	2G	5G
Cottage cheese	2G	5G	2G
Cream Cheese	2G	3G	10G
Mascarpone	1G	3G	14G
Mozzarella	2G	6G	6G
Brie	1G	7G	9G
Aged Cheddar	1G	8G	10G
Parmesan	2G	11G	8G

NUTS AND SEEDS

Keto Nut Source (2 oz)	Carbohydrates	Proteins	Fats
Macadamia Nuts	4G	5G	44G
Brazil Nuts	4G	9G	38G
Pecans	4G	6G	42G
Almonds	4G	11G	27G
Hazelnuts	4G	10G	37G

KETO NUT BAKING SOURCES

Keto Nut/Seed Baking Source (2OZ)	Carbohydrates	Proteins	Fats
Almond Flour	7G	12G	27G
Coconut Flour	7G	5G	5G
Chia Seed Meal	4G	9G	18G
Flaxseed Meal	2G	9G	19G
Unsweetened Coconut	9G	5G	41G

WATER AND BEVERAGE

WATER. This will be your main source of staying hydrated.

BROTH. This is full of electrolytes, vitamins and nutrients. It will kick start your day and give you energy.

COFFEE. It is perfectly fine with Keto diet, until and unless it is made with milk. Avoid milk coffee, drink black or use cream instead of milk.

TEA. Same principles apply here as that of coffee, try to drink black or green.

ALMOND MILK. You can use the unsweetened versions.

COCONUT MILK. You can use the unsweetened versions.

DIET SODA. Try not to drink this, it leads to sugar cravings, which is really harmful on keto diet.

ALCOHOL. Avoid beer at all costs, it is full of carbohydrates. Drink hard liquor if you want to.

KETOGENIC DIET MACROS

Macros play very important role in any type of diet you follow. Macros are main source of calories in your diet.

General macros for Ketogenic diet are 70% fats, 25 % protein and 5 % carbohydrates.

Whatever amount of calories you are taking, you should ensure that 70% of them are coming from fats, 25 % from proteins and 5 % from carbohydrates. This is the perfect macros for ketogenic diet, but if you don't get it perfect than don't worry, you are just a human and can't be perfect all the time. Just try your best to follow this macros and if you fail following this macros than don't quit on your diet, forgive yourself because everyone makes mistakes.

CHAPTER 5

GETTING STARTED WITH KETOGENIC DIET

Planning meals in advance.

Make sure that you are planning your meals in advance, this keeps you on track and you don't lose the sight of your goal.

Macros.

Make sure that you are taking 70% of your calories from fats, 25 % from proteins and 5% from carbohydrates.

Drink lots of water.

This will keep you hydrated and keep you full, drinking lots of water in any type of diet is helpful. No matter what kind of diet you are following, always drink lots of water.

7-8 hours of sleep

Sleep is an indispensable part of Ketogenic diet. Sleep recovers your body fully.

Vegetables

Make sure that most of your carbohydrates comes from your vegetables.

You can dive right in just after calculating your macros and planning your meals.

But if you don't want to calculate macros or plan meals, you can still follow Keto diet. Just listen to your body and eat whenever you feel hungry. But because of this you will fall short on your macros.

CHAPTER 6

HOW TO REACH KETOSIS

Reaching the state of ketosis might take few days, it completely depends on person to person. Reaching the state of ketosis will be your first success.

Following steps will help you reaching ketosis much faster;

Carbohydrates.

Take 20-50 grams of carbohydrates every day, make sure you are not eating more than 50 grams otherwise you will have high glucose levels which will stop you from reaching ketosis.

Proteins.

This is not a low carbohydrate high protein diet, you cannot eat high amounts of proteins in this diet, you have to take moderate servings of proteins in this diet. Usually 25 % of your entire calories.

Stop worrying about fats.

Eat fats and don't worry that they will make you fat, it is normal to have that kind of thoughts because we have been conditioned by society like this only. Eat healthy fats and turn into a fat burning machine, this is the beauty of ketogenic diet.

Water.

Drink lots of water, you have to keep yourself hydrated. You can also drink water with lemon in it.

Snacking.

Try to avoid snacking because snacking might give you insulin spike, you don't want that because than losing weight might become difficult.

Intermittent Fasting.

Intermittent fasting is a great way to reduce your calories and keep your insulin levels low. In this type of fasting you eat only for 8 hours and fasts for 16 hours.

I will write another book on this topic soon; so stay tuned.

Exercise.

Exercising for 20-30 minutes per day will increase your metabolism and help you lose weight even faster.

1. Coconut ice cream

Ingredients

2 cups canned coconut milk

1/3 cup of erythritol, xylitol or sweetener of choice

1/8 teaspoon salt

1 1/2 teaspoon pure vanilla extract or vanilla pod paste

How to make coconut ice cream

1. Make sure you use canned coconut milk with full fat.

2. If you want, you can use the seeds of a vanilla bean instead of the extract.

3. To make keto ice cream: mix milk, sweetener, salt and vanilla extract.

4. If you have an ice cream maker, just churn according to the manufacturer's instructions.

5. If you want to make it without an ice cream machine, freeze the mixture in ice cube trays, then mix the frozen cubes in a high speed blender like a vitamix or thaw them enough to mix in a food processor or a regular blender.

6. Eat as it is or freeze for an hour or two for a firmer texture.

7. Due to the lack of preservatives or stabilizers, keto ice cream is best to consume within 1 day, but you can technically freeze leftovers for up to a month and thaw them before serving.

Total serving 4

NUTRITION (serving 1)

CALORIES	297
PROTEINS	4.9 g
FATS	37 g
CARBS	4.6 g

2. Chocolate mousse

Ingredients

16 ounces cream cheese

1/2 cup unsweetened cocoa powder

1 large avocado

1/4 teaspoon vanilla extract

3-6 tablespoons of desired sweetener

1/2 cup heavy whipping cream

90% dark chocolate, to garnish

How to make chocolate mousse?

1. Beat cream cheese until it becomes really smooth and creamy, slowly mix cocoa powder.

2. Add avocado and beat it nicely for 5 minutes until it becomes really creamy.

3. Add vanilla and sweetener, than beat it again until it becomes creamy and smooth.

4. In a separate bowl, pitch the heavy cream.

5. Place the whipped cream in the chocolate mixture and fold gently until it's incorporated.

6. Place the chocolate mousse in a piping bag and the tube in the desired containers.

7. Garnish with dark chocolate chips.

NUTRITION (96 gram)

CALORIES	268
PROTEINS	5 g
FATS	26 g
CARBS	5 g

3. Cookies and cream

Ingredients

Cookies crumbs

3/4 cup almond flour

1/4 cup cocoa powder

1/4 teaspoon baking powder

1/4 cup of erythritol

1/2 tea spoon of vanilla extract

1 1/2 teaspoon coconut oil, softened

1 egg, room temperature

Pinch of salt

Ice cream

2 1/2 cups whipped cream

1 tablespoon vanilla extract

1/2 cup of erythritol

1/2 cup unsweetened almond milk

How to make cookies and cream ice cream

1. Preheat the oven to 300 ° F. Line a circular 9-inch cake pan on baking paper and spray with oil of choice.

2. Sift the almond flour, cocoa powder, baking soda, erythritol and salt into a medium bowl and mix everything until it is smooth.

3. Add the vanilla extract and coconut oil and mix until the dough turns into crumbs.

4. Add the egg and mix until the cookie dough starts to stick and form a ball.

5. Put the dough into a separated cake pan and lightly press the dough with your fingers until it evenly covers the bottom of the pan.

6. Place the pan in the preheated oven and bake for 20 minutes or until the center of the cookie bounces back when pressed.

7. Once cooking is complete, remove the pan from the oven and let it cool.

8. Once the cookie is cool, break the cookie into small pieces.

9. In a large bowl, mix the whipped cream with an electric mixer.

10. Add the vanilla extract and erythritol and stir until well blended.

11. Pour the almond milk and mix until it re-thickens.

12. Place the cream mixture on the ice cream maker and churn until the ice cream retains its shape.

13. Gradually pour the crumbled biscuit in the ice cream machine.

14. Once all the biscuits have been incorporated, place the ice cream in a ½-gallon container suitable for the freezer and freeze for at least 2 hours before serving.

Total servings 10

NUTRITION (1 serving)

CALORIES	239
PROTEINS	4.6 g
FATS	29 g
CARBS	4.7 g

4. Vanilla chia pudding

Ingredients

1 cup strawberries

Sweetener

Vanilla extract (few drops)

2 tablespoon of MCT oil

2 cup water

½ cup heavy cream

½ cup chia seeds

How to make vanilla chia pudding

1. Add chia seeds, heavy cream, water, MCT oil, vanilla extract and sweetener in a bowl.

2. Mix them together.

3. Allow to sit for 7-11 hours

4. After 11 hours add strawberries.

5. Your dish is ready.

Total servings 3

NUTRITION (1 serving)

CALORIES	297
PROTEINS	8 g
FATS	35 g
CARBS	5 g

5. Chocolate ice cream

Ingredients

5.3 oz (150 g) 85% or 90% dark chocolate, broken into pieces

1.8 oz (50 g) of cocoa butter

4 big eggs, separated

¼ teaspoon of tartar

½ cup Erythritol or Swerve Powder (80 g / 2.8 oz)

1 tablespoon of vanilla extract without sugar (15 ml)

1 ¼ cup thick cream or coconut cream (300 ml / 10,1 fl. Oz.)

How to cook chocolate ice cream

1. Melt chocolate and cocoa butter in a microwavable bowl.

2. Allow the melted chocolate to cool to room temperature.

3. In the meantime, separate the egg white from the egg yolk.

4. With an electric blender, beat egg whites and tartar. As the whites thicken, slowly add the powdered erythritol. Beat until they produce stiff peaks.

5. In another bowl beat the cream until soft peaks are obtained.

6. In a third bowl, mix the yolks with the vanilla extract.

7. When the chocolate has cooled to room temperature, add about one third of the egg whites using a rubber spatula and mix with the chocolate.

8. Add the remaining egg whites and fold gently without deflating.

9. Slowly stir in the egg yolk-vanilla mixture.

10. Finally, add the whipped cream to the spatula and make a soft chocolate mousse.

11. Transfer the chocolate mousse to a deep baking dish. Freeze for at least 4 to 6 hours or until the mixture is ready.

Total servings 5

NUTRITION (1 serving)

CALORIES	245
PROTEINS	2 g
FATS	32 g
CARBS	4 g

6. Chocolate chia pudding with almonds

Ingredients

4 tablespoon chopped almonds

Sweetener

2 tablespoon cocoa powder

2 tablespoon MCT oil

1 cup water

½ cup heavy cream

6 tablespoon chia seeds

How to make chocolate chia pudding with almonds

1. Add chia seeds, heavy cream, water, MCT oil, cocoa powder and sweetener in a bowl.

2. Mix them together.

3. Allow to sit for 7-11 hours

4. After 11 hours, add almonds.

5. Your dish is ready.

Total servings 3

NUTRITION (1 serving)

CALORIES	288
PROTEINS	4 g
FATS	36 g
CARBS	5 g

7. Pecan ice cream

Ingredients

1/4 cup butter

2 cups heavy cream

1/2 cup of swirve sweeteners

1/4 teaspoon salt

2 egg yolks

2 tablespoon maple extract

1 tablespoon sweetener

1 tablespoon of MCT oil

2 tablespoons of roasted pecans, chopped

How to make pecan ice cream

1. Melt butter, cream, sweetener and salt in a small saucepan.

2. Whisk the yolks until light. Take a spoonful of yolk and stir in the mixture to soften it.

3. Continue with a few more tablespoons and gradually add the remaining yellow in the mixture over the heat.

4. Continue stirring until the mixture thickens. Pour into a bowl to cool in the refrigerator for 30 minutes.

5. Then add maple extract, sweetener and MCT oil.

6. Combine the mixture in your ice cream maker. Follow the manufacturer's instructions.

7. Stir in the pecans and spread the ice in an 8 x 5 loaf pan and freeze for 2 to 3 hours to get a soft portion.

8. Your ice cream is ready.

Total servings 4

NUTRITION (1 serving)

CALORIES	355
PROTEINS	6 g
FATS	47 g
CARBS	7 g

8. Coconut Macadamia Chia Pudding

Ingredients

4 tablespoon macadamia nuts (chopped)

Sweetener

2 tablespoon MCT oil

1 cup water

½ cup coconut cream

6 tablespoon chia seeds

How to make coconut macadamia chia pudding

1. Add chia seeds, coconut cream, water, MCT oil and sweetener in a bowl.

2. Mix them together.

3. Allow to sit for 7-11 hours

4. After 11 hours add macadamia nuts.

5. Your dish is ready.

Total servings 3

NUTRITION (1 serving)

CALORIES	271
PROTEINS	5 g
FATS	33 g
CARBS	5 g

9. Strawberry ice cream

Ingredients

12 ounces of strawberries

1/2 cup Swerve sweetener

1 1/2 cups of sour cream

1 teaspoon of vanilla extract

1 1/2 cups of heavy cream

How to make strawberry ice cream

1. Place the strawberries and 1/4 of the sweetener in a blender or food processor. Blend until the puree is almost finished, but there are still small pieces.

2. In a large bowl, combine the sour cream, vanilla extract and strawberry mixture until smooth.

3. In another large bowl, mix the cream with the 1/4 cup of sweetener until it is very stiff.

4. Gently stir the whipped cream into the strawberry mixture.

5. Transfer to an airtight container and freeze for at least 6 hours.

Total servings 6

NUTRITION (1 serving)

CALORIES	220
PROTEINS	7 g
FATS	27 g
CARBS	2 g

10. Pumpkin chia spice pudding

Ingredients

4 tablespoon chopped roasted cashews

Pinch of cloves, nutmeg, ginger and cinnamon

2 tablespoon caramel syrup (sugar free)

6 tablespoon pumpkin puree

2 tablespoon MCT oil

2 cups of water

½ cup heavy cream

6 tablespoons chia seeds

How to cook pumpkin chia spice pudding

1. Add chia seeds, heavy cream, water, MCT oil, pumpkin puree, cinnamon, ginger, nutmeg, cloves and sweetener in a bowl.

2. Mix them together.

3. Allow it to sit for 7-11 hours

4. After 11 hours, add roasted cashews.

5. Your dish is ready.

Total servings 4

NUTRITION (1 serving)

CALORIES	235
PROTEINS	5 g
FATS	29 g
CARBS	3 g

11. Vanilla ice cream

Ingredients

4 cups heavy whipped cream

3 eggs yolk

4 teaspoons of beef gelatin

2 tablespoons of pure vanilla extract

1 whole vanilla bean scraped (optional)

1/4 teaspoon sea salt

1/2 cup to 1 cup sugar-free sweetener

How to make vanilla ice cream

1. Place the bowl of your ice cream maker in the freezer and freeze overnight. Note: If you do not have an ice cream maker, no problem! You can always make this recipe.

2. Put all the ingredients in a medium saucepan and whisk well. Note: Be sure to open the vanilla bean and scrape it in the mixture before adding the full bean, this will give you a lot of vanilla flavor.

4. Place the pan on heat on medium flame level. Cook and stir until the mixture begins to steam but is not completely boiled.

5. Remove from heat and allow the mixture to cool before transferring to a sealable container. Allow to cool for at least 2 hours or until completely cooled.

6. Stir the ice cream and place it in the ice cream maker.

7. Turn on the ice machine and stir until it is very thick and creamy.

8. Serve immediately for a soft consistency of ice cream. Transfer to a container that can be sealed and freeze for at least 2 hours.

Note: If you do not have an ice cream maker, simply transfer the base into a freezer and freeze for 4 hours or until it is completely frozen.

Total servings 8

NUTRITION (1 serving)

CALORIES	235
PROTEINS	2 g
FATS	29 g
CARBS	2 g

12. Keto blueberry muffins

Cream ingredients

1 Stick butter

8 tablespoons fresh cheese

1 Vanilla teaspoon

Dry ingredients
1 Cup coconut fibres

2 teaspoon baking soda

1/2 teaspoon salt

1/8 teaspoon cinnamon

1/4 teaspoon Xanthan chewing gum

Wet Ingredients

6 medium eggs

1/2 Cup heavy cream

And the Last

¾ cup blueberries

4 teaspoons coffee

How to make keto muffins

1. Mix butter, vanilla and cream cheese in a bowl, add 2 eggs and beat the mixture again.

2. Now add 1/3rd of the dry ingredients and mix until fully incorporated.

3. Add 2 more eggs and half of dry ingredients and beat the mixture again.

4. Now add last 2 eggs and remaining of the dry ingredients and mix them properly.

5. Finish the mixture by adding heavy cream and mix it properly until fully incorporated.

6. Add the berries and mix again.

7. Now fill them in muffin containers and bake them for 30 minutes at 400F.

8. Your muffins are ready.

Total servings 8

NUTRITION (1 serving)

CALORIES	250
PROTEINS	10.1 g
FATS	28 g
CARBS	3.4 g

13. Pumpkin pecan pie ice

Ingredients

1/2 cup of cottage cheese

1/2 cup of pumpkin purée

1 teaspoon. Pumpkin spice

2 cups of coconut milk

3 large egg yolks

1/2 teaspoon of xanthan gum

1/3 cup of erythritol

20 drops of liquid stevia

1 teaspoon maple extract

1/2 cup grilled and chopped pecans

2 tablespoon of salted butter

How to make pumpkin pecan pie ice cream

1. Chop the roasted pecans and put on stove with butter.

2. Put the other ingredients in a blender and blend until smooth.

3. Add the mixture to your ice cream maker.

4. Then add the pecans and butter.

5. Follow the brewing instructions according to the manufacturer's instructions for your ice machine.

6. Have fun!

Total servings 6

NUTRITION (1 serving)

CALORIES	187
PROTEINS	1 g
FATS	25 g
CARBS	2 g

14 Keto vanilla pound cake

Ingredients

2 cups almond flour

1/2 cup butter

1 cup of erythritol

2 teaspoons of baking powder

1 teaspoon of vanilla extract

1 cup of sour cream

2 ounces of cream cheese

4 big eggs

How to make Keto vanilla pound cake

1. Preheat the oven to 350 degrees Fahrenheit

2. Butter generously 9-inch pan, set aside

3. Combine almond flour and baking powder in a large bowl, set aside

4. Cut the butter into several small squares and place in a separate bowl, add the cream cheese

5. Microwave butter and cream cheese for 30 seconds. Be careful not to burn the cream cheese. Mix these ingredients until well combined.

6. Add erythritol, vanilla extract and sour cream to the butter and cream cheese mixture. Mix well.

7. Pour the wet ingredients into a large bowl of almond flour and baking soda. Mix well.

8. Add the eggs to the dough. Mix well.

9. Place the dough in the butter pan, and bake for 50 minutes.

10. For best results, allow the cake to cool completely for at least 2 hours, preferably overnight. If you remove it too soon, it may collapse a bit.

Total servings 12

NUTRITION (1 serving)

CALORIES	250
PROTEINS	15 g
FATS	25 g
CARBS	6 g

15. Keto mocha ice cream

Ingredients

1 cup of coconut milk

1/4 cup of heavy cream

2 tablespoon of erythritol

15 drops of liquid stevia

2 tablespoon of cocoa powder

1 tablespoon of instant coffee

1/4 teaspoon xanthan gum

How to make mocha ice cream

1. Put all ingredients except xanthan in a container and mix with a blender.

2. Slowly add the xanthan gum until a slightly thicker mixture is obtained.

3. Add to your ice cream maker and follow the manufacturer's instructions.

Total servings 2

NUTRITION (1 serving)

CALORIES	175
PROTEINS	3 g
FATS	15 g
CARBS	7 g

16 Keto chocolate mug

Ingredients

2 tablespoon butter

1/4 cup almond powder

2 tablespoon cocoa powder

1 big beaten egg

2 tablespoon Keto-based chocolate chips

1 teaspoon sweetener

1/2 teaspoon baking powder

Pinch kosher salt

1/4 cup Whipped cream, to serve

How to make keto chocolate mug

1. Put the butter in a microwaveable cup and heat until melted for 30 seconds.

2. Add remaining ingredients except whipped cream and stir well.

3. Microwave for 45 seconds to 1 minute, or until the cake is set, but still fudgy.

4. Serve with cream.

NUTRITION (1 serving)

CALORIES	405
PROTEINS	13 g
FATS	37 g
CARBS	6 g

17. Butterscotch sea salt ice cream

Ingredients
1 cup of coconut milk

1/4 cup sour cream

1/4 cup heavy cream

3 table spoon Butter

2 tablespoon vodka

2 teaspoons of butterscotch flavor

25 drops of liquid stevia

2 tbsp. erythritol

1/2 teaspoon of xanthan gum

1 teaspoon sea salt

How to make butterscotch sea salt ice cream

1. Put all the ingredients in a container and mix with a hand blender.

2. Add to the ice maker and follow the manufacturer's instructions.

Total servings 3

NUTRITION (1 serving)

CALORIES	274
PROTEINS	2 g
FATS	25 g
CARBS	4 g

18 No Bake Low Carb Lemon Strawberry Cheesecake

Ingredients

3 ounces of cream cheese,

3/4 cup heavy whipped cream

1/3 cup sweetener

2 teaspoons lemon extract

Zest of 1 lemon

2 big strawberries

How to make no Bake Low Carb Lemon Strawberry Cheesecake Treats

1. Add cream cheese, sweetener and whipped cream in a bowl. Beat it at high speed until smooth and creamy.

2. Add lemon extract and mix.

3. Take 1 strawberry and chop it into small pieces. Cut the other strawberry in thin pieces in the shape of a heart.

4. Fill half of each jar with half of the cream cheese mixture.

5. Add the chopped strawberry to the jars to get a nice layer.

6. Cover the strawberries with rest of the cream cheese mixture.

7. Use the strawberry slices to create a flow pattern on top.

8. Sprinkle with the lemon zest in the center of each flower.

9. Cool in refrigerator.

10. Your dessert is ready

Total servings 2

NUTRITION (1 serving)

CALORIES	374
PROTEINS	4.5 g
FATS	48.2 g
CARBS	5.7 g

19. Chocolate Chunk Avocado Ice Cream

Ingredients

2 middle size avocados

1 cup of coconut milk

1/2 cup heavy cream

1/2 cup cocoa powder

2 teaspoons of vanilla extract

1/2 cup powdered erythritol

25 drops of liquid stevia

6 squares unsweetened bakers chocolate

How to cook Chocolate Chunk Avocado Ice Cream

1. Add the avocado in a bowl, add the coconut milk, cream and the vanilla extract.

2. Use a hand blender to mix it into a creamy substance.

3. Powder erythritol in a spice grinder.

4. Then add erythritol, stevia and cocoa powder to the avocado mixture.

5. Mix well, then chop the chocolate and add it to the bowl.

6. Leave the bowl in the refrigerator for 6-12 hours, then about 20 minutes before serving, add the mixture to the ice cream maker and prepare according to the manufacturer's instructions.

Total servings 6

NUTRITION (1 serving)

CALORIES	203
PROTEINS	3.8 g
FATS	25g
CARBS	3.7 g

20. Strawberry Rhubarb Ice Cream

Ingredients

5 egg yolks

½ cup of Swerve (or desired sweetness)

1 cup heavy whipped cream

1 cup unsweetened vanilla milk almond

½ cup rhubarb diced

2 teaspoons of strawberry extract

¼ teaspoon of fine-grained sea salt

How to make Strawberry Rhubarb Ice Cream

1. Put all ingredients in a blender and blend until smooth.

2. Taste and adjust the sweetness and flavor of strawberry to your taste.

3. Put them in your ice cream maker and follow the instructions of your ice cream maker.

4. Freeze until adjustment.

5. Your ice cream is ready

Total servings 5

NUTRITION (1 serving)

CALORIES	186
PROTEINS	3.8 g
FATS	22 g
CARBS	4.25 g

21. Keto oven-baked Brie cheese

Ingredients

9 ounces of brie or Camembert cheese

2 ounces of pecan or walnut

1 clove of garlic

1 tablespoon of fresh rosemary or fresh thyme or fresh parsley

1 tablespoon of olive oil

salt and pepper

How to make Keto oven-baked Brie cheese

1. Preheat the oven to 400 ° F (200 ° C).

2. Place the cheese on a baking sheet lined with baking paper or in a small non-stick pan.

3. Chop the garlic and roughly chop the nuts and herbs.

4. Mix the three together with the olive oil.

5. Add salt and pepper.

6. Put the walnut mixture over the cheese and bake for 10 minutes or until the cheese is lukewarm and soft and the nuts are toasted.

7. Serve warm or tepid.

Total servings 4

NUTRITION (1 serving)

CALORIES	274
PROTEINS	14 g
FATS	31 g
CARBS	1 g

22. Avocado pops

Ingredients

3 ripe avocados

Juice of 2 limes

3 tablespoon Swerve or other alternative to sugar

3/4 cup. coconut milk

1 tablespoon. coconut oil

1 cup keto friendly Chocolate-

How to make avocado pops

1. Mix the avocados in a blender or food processor with the lime juice, swerve and coconut milk. Mix until smooth and pour into the Popsicle mold.

2. Freeze until firm, (6 hours to overnight.)

3. In a medium bowl mix chocolate pieces and coconut oil. Microwave until it melts, then cool to room temperature. Dunk pops in chocolate and serve.

NUTRITION (1 serving)

CALORIES	62
PROTEINS	1 g
FATS	7 g
CARBS	2 g

23 Pecan cheesecake

Ingredients

2 cups almond flour

3 tablespoons butter

½ teaspoon vanilla (optional)

1 cup of sugar Swerve

2 eggs

8 oz of cream cheese

½ to 1 teaspoon of maple extract

1 cup of pecans and two tablespoons for garnishing

How to make pecan cheesecake

1. Melt butter and mix with flour, vanilla and swerve.

2. Stir in the egg yolk (1 egg).

3. Insert in tart pan by pressing with your fingers.

4. Bake for 10 minutes at 350 degrees F.

5. Make filling

6. Mix Cream cheese with vanilla, maple extract and egg. Start with ½ teaspoon extract.

7. Chop pecans. Mix with a little sea salt.

8. Put the pecans first (though you can reverse what you want)

9. Pour cheesecake mixture.

10 Garnish with two tablespoons of pecans.

11. Bake for 20 minutes at 350 degrees F or until the cream cheese mixture is set.

12. Cool completely.

13. Cool for at least six hours, preferably overnight.

14. Cut into 16 squares.

Total servings 16
NUTRITION (1 serving)

CALORIES	150
PROTEINS	5.89 g
FATS	18 g
CARBS	2 g

24. Lemon ice cream

Ingredients

1 lemon, peel and juice

3 eggs

1/3 cup of erythritol

1¾ cup heavy whipped cream

¼ teaspoon yellow food coloring

How to make lemon ice cream

1. Wash the lemon in warm water. Finely grate (peel) the outer skin. Extract the juice and set aside.

2. Separate the eggs. Beat the egg whites until firm. Beat egg yolk and sweetener until foamy in another bowl. Add lemon juice and a few drops of yellow food coloring (optional). Carefully stir the egg white into the yolk mixture.

3. Beat the cream in a large bowl until soft peaks form. Stir in the egg mixture with cream.

4. Put in the ice cream maker and freeze according to the manufacturer's instructions.

5. If you do not have an ice cream maker, you can place the bowl in the freezer and mix every half hour until the desired consistency is achieved.

6. It can take up to 2 hours. Use a spatula to scrape the inside of the bowl while stirring. When frozen, allow to stand at room temperature for 15 minutes before serving.

Total serving 4

NUTRITION (1 serving)

CALORIES	210
PROTEINS	5 g
FATS	23 g
CARBS	3 g

25 Coconut cookies

Ingredients

3 cups of unsweetened coconut flakes

1 cup coconut oil,

1/2 cup sweet maple syrup

How to make coconut cookies

1. Lay out a large plate or baking tray with parchment paper and set aside.

2. In a large bowl mix all ingredients and mix well. Lightly moisten the hands, then form small balls with the dough and place them on the baking tray at a distance of 1 to 2 inches.

3. Tap on each biscuit with a fork. Cool until firm.

NUTRITION (1 cookie)

CALORIES	99
PROTEINS	3 g
FATS	10 g
CARBS	2 g

If you are really enjoying this book or find it useful. I'd be really grateful if you write short review on Amazon. Your support really does make a difference and I read all your reviews personally. So I can get your feedback and make this book even better.

If you would like to leave a review all you have to do is go to amazon and type keto desserts by Shahrukh Akhtar and leave a review.

Thanks a lot for your support.

26. Almond Roll with Pumpkin Cream Cheese Filling

Ingredients

For the cake

130 grams of egg whites

120 grams of mixed erythritol / stevia powder, divided

120 grams of almond flour

4 grams of pure almond extract

To fill the pumpkin

300 grams cream cheese, soft but fresh

71 grams of salted butter, softened

61 grams of powdered erythritol / stevia mixture

1 teaspoon pure vanilla pod paste

2 teaspoons of pumpkin spices

180 grams of pumpkin puree

How to make Almond Roll with Pumpkin Cream Cheese Filling

For the cake

1. Preheat the oven to 400F.

2. In a bowl add mixture of egg whites and 56 g sweetener.

3. Use a whisk to beat.

4. In another bowl mix the remaining 56 g of sweetener, almond flour and flavor.

5. Whisk to homogeneity.

6. Carefully mix the dry mixture into the egg whites.

7. Spread the dough evenly on a baking sheet covered with grease and parchment paper (or baking sheet).

8. Bake for 11-13 minutes. Invert on a grid covered with parchment paper to cool.

To fill the pumpkin

1. Beat the cream cheese in a medium bowl until smooth.

2. Add the sweetener. Continue until fluffy and light.

3. Add the vanilla paste and pumpkin spices. Beat until well installed.

4. Add the pumpkin puree in two intervals.

5. Add the butter and beat until the mixture is mixed evenly. Your filling should be smooth and light.

6. Keep cool until served.

Assembly

Spread the filling evenly on the sponge.

Carefully roll into a log, use the parchment to lift the cake. I find that rolling the cake on the short side results in a thicker and less sharp roll. Keep cool until served.

Total servings 10

NUTRITION (1 serving)

CALORIES	230
PROTEINS	4.76 g
FATS	27 g
CARBS	3.5 g

27. Orange Cake Balls

Ingredients

2/3 cup almond butter

1/3 cup coconut flour

Zest of 2 navel oranges

1/4 cup of orange juice

35 drops of sweet cream with vanilla to taste

1/2 teaspoon of vanilla

Pinch of pink salt

How to make Orange Cake Balls

1. Mix all ingredients in a mixing bowl. Mix well.

2. Adjust if needed - If too dry, add a little orange juice or a dash of avocado oil. If it is too moist, add some coconut flour.

3. Make balls with a small biscuit spoon. Use palms to gently press and fit.

4. Lightly roll each ball into a small bowl of coconut flour (about 1-2 pounds). Optional - freeze or refrigerate for 10 minutes if desired. Enjoy

Total servings 6

NUTRITION (1 serving)

CALORIES	92
PROTEINS	3 g
FATS	9 g
CARBS	4 g

28 Carrot Cake Keto Balls

Ingredients

1 block of 8 ounces cream cheese, made soft

3/4 cup coconut flour

1 teaspoon stevia

1/2 teaspoon pure vanilla extract

1 teaspoon of cinnamon

1/4 teaspoon ground nutmeg

1 cup of grated carrots

1/2 cup chopped pecans

1 cup shredded unsweetened coconut

How to make Carrot Cake Keto Balls

1. Whisk the cream cheese, coconut flour, stevia, vanilla, cinnamon and nutmeg in a large bowl with a whisk. Stir in the carrots and pecans.

2. Roll in 16 balls, then roll in the grated coconut and serve.

Total servings 16

NUTRITION (1 serving)

CALORIES	85
PROTEINS	4 g
FATS	8 g
CARBS	5 g

29. Sugar Free "Mounds" Fudge

Ingredients

1/2 cup of coconut butter

1 tablespoon pure coconut oil

2 tablespoons sweetener

2 tablespoons unsweetened coconut finely shredded

1/4 cup heavy whipped cream

How to make Sugar Free "Mounds" Fudge

1. In a 9-cavity silicone pan, add 1-2 tablespoons of fudge mixture in Cavity, then harden it in the freezer.

2. In the meantime, heat 1/2 cup coconut butter until soft.

3. Add the melted coconut oil, sweetener, coconut, heavy cream and mix well.

4. After the fudge is firm (about 20 minutes), add coconut mixture to cover the fudge in each cavity.

5. Put in the freezer for 10-15 minutes.

6. Put the rest of the fudge on top of the coconut mix and put it back in the freezer to completely harden it

7. Remove from the silicone mold and cut into pieces.

8. Your dessert is ready.
Total servings 4

NUTRITION (1 serving)

CALORIES	220
PROTEINS	5 g
FATS	25 g
CARBS	3 g

30. Nuts fat bombs with apples

Ingredients

75 g of fat cream cheese

1 tablespoon butter

½ green apple

1/6 teaspoon garlic powder

1/6 teaspoon onion powder

35 gram walnuts

Pinch salt and pepper

How to make nut fat bombs with apples

1. Place butter and cream cheese in a blender and blend them until smooth.

2. Chop apple into small bites.

3. Add onion and garlic powder, in the creamy mixture.

4. Add salt, pepper and stir it nicely.

5. Cut nuts into pieces and place them in the mixture.

6. Form balls out of the mixture and put them in refrigerator for 3 hours.

Total servings 6

NUTRITION (1 serving)

CALORIES	134
PROTEINS	5 g
FATS	15g
CARBS	2 g

31. Granola fat bombs

Ingredients

1/3 cup of macadamia nuts

1 egg

3 tablespoon coconut oil

1 ½ tablespoon of vanilla extract

1/3 cup chocolate chips.

3 tablespoon peanut butter

1/3 cup of coconut chips

1/3 cup of sunflower seeds

1/3 cup of almonds

How to make granola fat bombs

1. Preheat the oven at 200 degrees.

2. Place all the ingredients in a blender, and blend properly until smooth.

3. Place the mixture in a baking dish and bake for 16 - 20 minutes until the color turns golden brown.

4. Take out the baking dish cool it and serve.

Total servings 7

NUTRITION (1 serving)

CALORIES	180
PROTEINS	7 g
FATS	21g
CARBS	3 g

32. Macadamia Nut Fat Bomb

Ingredients

½ cup coconut oil

3 tablespoon cocoa powder

3 tablespoon erythritol

1 and ½ teaspoon vanilla extract

15 macadamia nuts

Pinch salt

How to cook macadamia nut fat bomb

1. In a medium bowl mix together cocoa powder, coconut oil, sweetener and vanilla extract until smooth.

2. Take a small container with parchment paper. Container size should be 4 x 6. Pour in chocolate mix.

3. Place nuts in chocolate mix.

4. Now place the container in freezer for 20 minutes.

5. Remove the container and cut it into 6 equal pieces.

7. Your macadamia nut fat bombs are ready.

Total servings 5

NUTRITION (1 serving)

CALORIES	95
PROTEINS	7 g
FATS	8 g
CARBS	2 g

33. Fat bomb fudge

Ingredients

8 tablespoon whip cream

½ cup Dark chocolate

2 tablespoon Irish butter

4 oz cream cheese

How to make fat bomb fudge

1. In a pan melt butter by heating it on low flame.

2. Add cream cheese to the butter.

3. Remove the mixture from pan and add it to a bowl.

4. Add heavy cream to the mixture.

5. Add chocolate chips.

6. Put in freezer for 1 hour.

7. Your fat bombs are ready.

Total servings 10

NUTRITION (1 serving)

CALORIES	120
PROTEINS	6 g
FATS	12 g
CARBS	3 g

34. Peanut butter white chocolate cups

Ingredients

½ cup cocoa butter

2 tablespoon peanut butter

1/3 tablespoon coconut oil

1 tablespoon coconut milk

½ teaspoon vanilla extract

Pinch salt

1 teaspoon honey

Few drops of stevia

How to make peanut butter white chocolate cups

1. In a pan, heat coconut oil, peanut butter, cocoa butter and coconut milk.

2. Whisk properly until smooth.

3. Remove pan from heat, now add vanilla extract, salt and sweetener.

4. Pour the mixture into molds and freeze them for 1 hour.

5. Your fat bombs are ready.

Total servings 6

NUTRITION (1 serving)

CALORIES	150
PROTEINS	6 g
FATS	16 g
CARBS	4 g

35. Pecan fudge fat bomb

Ingredients

2 oz cocoa butter

¼ cup coconut oil

2 tablespoon cocoa powder

2 tablespoon erythritol

¼ cup heavy cream

¼ cup pecan

How to make pecan fudge fat bombs

1. Melt cocoa butter and coconut oil together in a pan.

2. Add cocoa powder and whisk it properly.

3. Pour the mixture in a blender.

4. Add erythritol and blend properly.

5. Add cream and blend again.

6. Fill molds with pecan (half).

7. Pour the mixture in the molds.

8. Put in freezer for 2 hours.

9. Your pecan fat bombs are ready.

Total servings 8

NUTRITION (1 serving)

CALORIES	120
PROTEINS	5 g
FATS	13g
CARBS	3 g

36. Almond butter fat bomb

Ingredients

½ cup almond butter

½ cup coconut oil

4 tablespoon cocoa powder

½ cup erythritol

How to make almond butter fat bombs

1. In a medium bowl mix together almond butter and coconut oil.

2. Microwave it for 20-35 seconds.

3. Whisk it properly so that it becomes smooth.

4. Add cocoa powder and erythritol.

5. Pour the mixture into molds.

6. Put in the freezer for 20 minutes.

Total servings 7

NUTRITION (1 serving)

CALORIES	124
PROTEINS	4 g
FATS	13 g
CARBS	2 g

37. Chocolate peanut butter keto cup

Ingredients

2 cup coconut oil

1 cup peanut butter (natural)

4 tablespoon heavy cream

2 tablespoon cocoa powder

2 teaspoon liquid stevia

1/2 teaspoon vanilla extract

1/2 teaspoon salt

2 oz salted peanuts

How to cook chocolate peanut butter keto cups

1. Heat the coconut oil in a frying pan, add peanut butter.

2. Stir until mixed well.

3. Add cocoa powder, stevia, vanilla extract, salt and heavy cream. Whisk it well.

4. Pour the mixture in muffin cup holder and pour the peanuts from top.

5. Freeze the containers for 40 minutes and enjoy your chocolate peanut butter cups.

Total servings 8

NUTRITION (1 serving)

CALORIES	226
PROTEINS	7 g
FATS	26 g
CARBS	2 g

38. White chocolate fat bomb

Ingredients

½ cup cocoa butter

2 tablespoon peanut butter

1 tablespoon coconut oil

1 tablespoon coconut milk

½ tablespoon vanilla extract

Pinch salt

1 teaspoon honey

Stevia (few drops)

How to make white chocolate fat bombs

1. In a pan add cocoa butter, peanut butter, coconut oil, and coconut milk, heat on very low flame until melted. Whisk well to combine.

2. Now turn off the heat and add vanilla paste and sweetener of your choice to taste.

3. Bring out your molds and pour the mixture in them.

4. Place the molds in the freezer for 30 minutes to 1 hour.

5. Enjoy your white chocolate fat bombs.

Total servings 8

NUTRITION (1 serving)

CALORIES	99
PROTEINS	7.8 g
FATS	9 g
CARBS	2.2 g

39. Blueberry buttermilk ice cream

Ingredients

Puree of the blueberry

1/2 pound (227 g) Blueberries

2 tablespoons (1 oz / 30 ml) lemon juice

1 tablespoon (1/2 oz / 15 ml) of water

1/4 cup (55 g) of erythritol

1/8 teaspoon cinnamon

1 pinch of freshly ground nutmeg

1/8 teaspoon almond extract

1/4 teaspoon vanilla extract

1/8 teaspoon stevia glycerite

Balsamic vinegar

1/4 cup (2 oz / 60 ml) balsamic vinegar

Buttermilk and blueberry ice cream base

1 1/2 cup (12 oz / 255 ml) heavy cream

1 1/8 cup (10 oz / 295 ml) buttermilk

1/3 cup (55 g) of erythritol

2 tablespoons vanilla vodka (1 oz / 30 ml)

1/4 teaspoon salt

1/2 teaspoon Stevia Glycerite

1 teaspoon (5 ml) reduction of balsamic vinegar

How to make blueberry buttermilk ice cream

For blueberry puree:
1. Weigh and wash the blueberries.

2. Put them in a small saucepan with 1 tablespoon of water, two tablespoons of lemon juice, cinnamon, nutmeg and 1/4 cup of erythritol.

3. Cook at medium heat until boiling, then reduce heat and simmer for another 10 minutes.

4. Put the softened blueberries in a blender and blend at low speed.

5. Pour the blueberry puree into the saucepan and simmer for another 20 to 30 minutes, stirring every few minutes. The blueberry puree must be syrupy, and have an intense flavor.

6. Remove the puree from heat and add stevia, almond extract and vanilla. Stir and cool it completely.

7. Can be refrigerated for up to a week.

To reduce the balsamic reduction:

1. Put 1/4 cup balsamic vinegar in a small saucepan and simmer until half is reduced. Cool.

2. Use 1 teaspoon in the recipe and the rest for more ice cream or pour it into the bottle.

Buttermilk and blueberry ice cream base preparation:

1. Add the blueberry puree and all the ingredients of the ice cream base to the jug of a blender. Blend until well mixed.

To make buttermilk and blueberry ice cream:

1. Follow the instructions as mentioned by your ice cream maker. Cover and place in the freezer.

2. Let stand on the counter for 15 minutes before serving to soften slightly.

Total servings 5
NUTRITION (1 serving)

CALORIES	155
PROTEINS	8 g
FATS	15 g
CARBS	2 g

40. Chocolate fat bombs

They are very tasty and great source of fats. They are very easy to make.

Ingredients

117g/4.1 Ounces Cream Cheese

117g/4.1 Ounces Unsalted Butter

2.5 Tablespoons Cacao Powder

1.5 Tablespoon Sweetener.

How to make chocolate fat bombs?

1. Place butter and cream cheese in a large bowl. Allow them to soften gently at room temperature.

2. Beat nicely with electric whisk once they soften.

3. Add your sweetener and cocoa powder.

4. Make it smooth by beating.

5. You will need mini baking cups or any container to give them shape.

6. Once mini baking cups are out, add 1-2 table spoon of mixture to these cups.

7. Place them in refrigerator and enjoy.

Total servings 8

NUTRITION (1 serving)

CALORIES	224
PROTEINS	7.8 g
FATS	13.2g
CARBS	6.2 g

41. Almond ice cream

Ingredients

6 tablespoons of butter

1/2 cup swirve sweetener

2 tablespoons of coconut sugar

1/2 teaspoon of vanilla extract

3/4 teaspoon Salt or sea salt

1 1/2 cup whipped cream

1 cup almonds or unsweetened cashew milk

4 large egg yolks

2 tablespoons of vodka (optional)

1/4 teaspoon Xanthan gum

3 ounces dark chocolate with no sugar.

Chocolate cocoa chopped

How to make almond ice cream

1. Place a medium bowl on an ice bath and set aside.

2. In a large pot mix butter, sweetener and coconut sugar.

3. When the butter has melted, stir well. Bring to a boil and cook for 3 to 5 minutes, making sure that it does not burn.

4. Remove from heat and stir in vanilla and salt.

5. Slowly add the cream while constantly stirring. Stir in almond milk.

6. Return to medium heat and cook, stirring often, until mixture reaches 170 ° F on an instant read thermometer.

7. Stir egg yolks into a medium bowl until smooth. Slowly add about 1 cup of hot cream mixture and wipe constantly. Then slowly add the egg yolk to the hot cream in the pan, stirring constantly. Continue cooking until the mixture reaches 180 ° F on an instant reading thermometer.

8. Put the vanilla pudding in the bowl on the ice bath and allow it to cool for 10 minutes. Then place well in plastic wrap and refrigerate for at least 2 hours.

9. Stir in the vodka, sprinkle with xanthan gum and stir vigorously. Pour the mixture into the cans of an ice cream maker and disassemble them according to the manufacturer's instructions.

10. After stirring, place half in an airtight container and sprinkle with half of the chopped chocolate. Garnish with remaining ice cream and chocolate and stir. Cover with plastic wrap, freeze for about 2 hours.

Total servings 8

NUTRITION (1 serving)

CALORIES	175
PROTEINS	7 g
FATS	19.3g
CARBS	3.2 g

42. Mint ice cream

Ingredients

Sugar-free mint ice cream

2 avocados

250 ml almond milk

250 ml double / heavy cream

100 g sweetener powder

1 tablespoon of lime juice / lemon

1 teaspoon mint extract

1/2 teaspoon of salt to taste

Sugar Free Magic Shell - Dairy Free

70 g of melted coconut oil

30 g unsweetened cocoa

70 g sweetener powder

1 teaspoon of vanilla

1/2 teaspoon of salt to taste

How to make mint ice cream

Sugar-free mint ice cream

1. Put all ingredients in a blender and mix until smooth.

2. Put into an ice cream maker and churn until it is frozen and light but creamy.

3. Serve immediately or freeze until needed.

4. You can keep it for 1 month in the freezer.

Sugar Free Magic Shell - Dairy Free

1. Put all ingredients in a bowl and stir until no more lumps are left.

2. Refrigerate for up to 2 weeks or freeze for 1 month. You need to warm it up before you use it.

Total servings 10

NUTRITION (1 serving)

CALORIES	175
PROTEINS	7.3 g
FATS	17.3g
CARBS	3.2 g

43. Death by chocolate

Ingredients

2 cups heavy cream

1 1/2 cup unsweetened cashew milk or almond or coconut,

1/2 cup cocoa powder for super dark ice cream

1/2 cup sweetener

4 large egg yolks

3 ounces chopped unsweetened chocolate

2 tablespoons of vodka (optional)

1/2 teaspoon vanilla extract

1/4 to 1/2 teaspoon liquid stevia extract or other sweetener, to taste

1/4 teaspoon xanthan (optional)

How to make death by chocolate ice cream

1. Put a bowl on an ice bath and set it aside.

2. In medium pan over medium heat mix cream, 1 cup cashew milk, cocoa powder and sweetener.

3. Stir until well mixed and stir until the mixture reaches 170 ° F on an Instant Read Thermometer.

4. Whisk egg yolks in a medium bowl. Slowly add 1 cup of hot cream mixture and whisk continuously to soften the egg yolk.

5. Slowly add egg yolks to the pan, stirring constantly. Bake and stir until the mixture reaches 175 ° F on an instant thermometer and is thick enough to coat the back of a spoon.

6. Remove from heat and add the chopped chocolate. Let stand for 5 minutes and then stir until smooth.

7. Put the mixture on an ice bath and allow it to cool for 10 minutes. Then wrap well in plastic wrap and refrigerate for at least 3 hours.

8. Whisk in 1/2 cup cashew milk, vodka, if available, vanilla extract and stevia extract (the mixture will be VERY thick until these ingredients are well incorporated).

9. Sprinkle the surface with xanthan gum, if used, and whisk vigorously to combine.

10. Pour the mixture into the cans of an ice cream maker and churn according to the manufacturer's instructions.

11. Once churned, you can serve immediately, or you can pack in an airtight container and freeze until a little firmer (1 to 2 hours).

Total servings 10
NUTRITION (1 serving)

CALORIES	133
PROTEINS	3 g
FATS	13 g
CARBS	3.9g

44. Lemon and buttermilk

Ingredients
1 cup buttermilk 8 oz / 227 g

1 cup heavy cream 8 oz / 227 g

1 cup almond milk 8 oz / 227 g

1/2 cup erythritol 115 g, sweetener of your choice

1/4 teaspoon Stevia Glycerite

2 tablespoons lemon juice 10 ml

Zest of lemon

Small pinch of salt

How to make lemon and buttermilk ice cream

1. Measure all ingredients into a blender and blend on low.

2. Pour the mixture into 16 small popsicle shapes and freeze.

3. Your pops are ready.

Total servings 10
NUTRITION (1 serving)

CALORIES	111
PROTEINS	6 g
FATS	14 g
CARBS	2 g

45. Orange popsicles

Ingredients

1 and a half cup (357 g) whipped cream

3/4 cup (180 g) almond milk, unsweetened,

2/3 cup (181 g) sugar-free orange marmalade

2 tablespoon "Swerve" or other sugar substitute

1 teaspoon (4 g) vanilla extract

Salt

How to make orange popsicles

1. Mix the ingredients in a medium bowl and make sure the sweetener is completely dissolved.

2. Pour the mixture into the molds. Place your sticks at the bottom of the molds and freeze until firm (about 6 hours).

3. To remove from mold, keep it under hot tap water for about 10 seconds. The pops are ready!

Total servings 6
NUTRITION (1 serving)

CALORIES	147
PROTEINS	6 g
FATS	14 g
CARBS	3 g

46. Vanilla pudding popsicles

Ingredients

1 cup whipped cream

1/2 cup unsweetened almond milk

3 large egg yolks

Sweetener is equivalent to 6 tablespoons of sugar

pinch of salt

2 tablespoons butter, cut into two pieces

1 1/2 teaspoons of vanilla extract

1/4 teaspoon Xanthan gum

How to make vanilla pudding popsicles

1. Mix Whip cream and almond milk in a medium saucepan over medium heat. Just bring it to simmer.

2. Whisk egg yolk with sweetener and salt in a medium bowl.

3. Slowly mix half of the hot cream mixture into the egg yolk and whisk continuously.

4. Then slowly beat the yellow / creamy mixture in the pan and cook until thickened for 4 to 5 minutes.

5. Remove from heat and stir in butter and vanilla extract.

6. Sprinkle the surface with xanthan gum and whisk vigorously to combine.

7. Divide the mixture into the popsicles molds.

8. Freeze for one hour, then press the wooden sticks mid-way into the frozen lollipops. Continue to freeze for at least 6 hours.

Total servings 5
NUTRITION (1 serving)

CALORIES	182
PROTEINS	6 g
FATS	21 g
CARBS	6 g

47. Peanut butter popsicles

Ingredients

2 cans of 13.5 ounces of coconut milk

1/2 cup peanut butter

1 teaspoon of liquid stevia

How to make peanut butter popsicles

1. Put the ingredients in a high-speed mixer and mix well.

2. Taste and adjust the sweetener if necessary.

3. Pour the mixture into the molds and freeze for 3 to 4 hours.

4. Your popsicles are ready.

Total servings 4

NUTRITION (1 serving)

CALORIES	163
PROTEINS	7 g
FATS	15.4g
CARBS	3.4g

About Author

Shahrukh Akhtar is the bestselling author of "Ketogenic Diet Simplified".

Shahrukh is an entrepreneur, motivational speaker, bodybuilder and an author.

He has competed in various bodybuilding competitions. He is a fitness expert.

Shahrukh's primary focus, through his books is to help everyone around the world to become fit, healthy and live a happy life.

ONE LAST THING

If you really enjoyed this book or find it useful. I'd be really grateful if you write short review on Amazon. Your support really does make a difference and I read all your reviews personally. So I can get your feedback and make this book even better.

If you would like to leave a review all you have to do is go to amazon and type keto desserts by Shahrukh Akhtar and leave a review.

Thanks a lot for your support.

Made in the USA
Columbia, SC
26 January 2019